My Cookie Business

Entrepreneurial Kids' Books

by
Dianne Linderman

Illustrated by
Dolores Uselman Johnson

KIDS'
Entrepreneurial
BOOKS

Story by
Dianne Linderman

Illustrations by
Dolores Uselman Johnson

Edited by
Elizabeth von Radics

Layout by
Dianne Linderman and Saga Design

Library of Congress Cataloging-in-Publication Data
ISBN 0-9704876-0-6

Published by
The First Moms' Club
205 Fern Valley Road, Suite N
Medford, Oregon 97501
www.thefirstmomsclub.com

Printed in the United States of America.

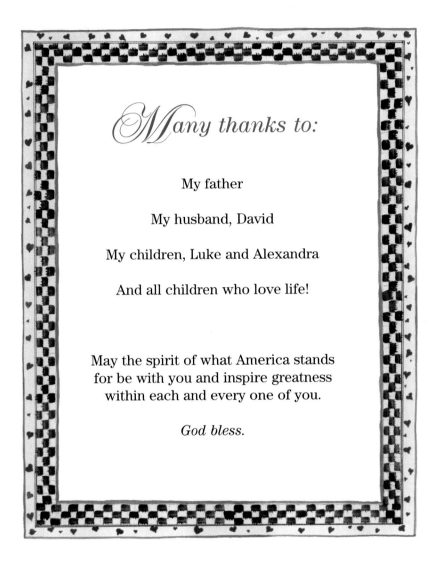

$\mathcal{M}$any thanks to:

My father

My husband, David

My children, Luke and Alexandra

And all children who love life!

May the spirit of what America stands
for be with you and inspire greatness
within each and every one of you.

God bless.

Every summer eleven-year-old Elizabeth visited her grandmother on Nantucket Island. She always looked forward to spending the whole summer with Nana in her big, beautiful, old Victorian-style home just off Main Street. Nana's backyard was a wide, sandy beach, where Elizabeth could play all summer, swimming in the ocean while Nana watched from the comfort of her large, old-fashioned beach chair.

Each afternoon, Nana and Elizabeth walked on the beach, looking for shells and tiny treasures that may have washed up on the shore. Elizabeth looked forward to coming back from their walk at four o'clock, because she and Nana always shared high tea on the front porch.

One day Nana said, "I am going to make my very special cookies for our tea, Elizabeth. Would you like to help me?"

"Yes!" Elizabeth exclaimed. So Elizabeth and Nana collected all the necessary ingredients for making "Nana's Chocolate Maple Sandcastles."

Nana's
Chocolate Maple Sandcastles

2	cups	Oat flour
1/4	cup	Whole-wheat flour
1	teaspoon	Baking soda
1	teaspoon	Salt
1 1/2	cups	Maple sugar or brown sugar
1	cup	Butter (2 sticks)
1	teaspoon	Pure vanilla extract
2	eggs	
2	cups	Semisweet chocolate morsels

This is an actual family recipe — please enjoy it.

"Put all of the ingredients together in a bowl and mix them carefully," said Nana, "and be sure not to overmix! Heat the oven to 375 degrees, please, Elizabeth."

Next, Nana and Elizabeth dropped the little "sandcastles" on the cookie sheets. They baked them for ten to twelve minutes until they were golden brown.

11

Soon the incredible aroma of chocolate-and-butter cookies permeated every room of the house and drifted out the windows.

Beachgoers lifted their noses into the air and were drawn toward Nana's house. A couple of people asked, "What is that *wonderful* smell?"

Nana's next-door neighbor, Mr. Jakes, said, "I am going to find out."

He knocked on the door and, when Nana and Elizabeth answered, he said, "Good day, Misses. I couldn't help smelling the delightful aroma of freshly baked goods coming from your kitchen. Could I inquire what it is and if I could purchase some?"

Nana was tickled that Mr. Jakes was so bold as to ask about the cookies. She answered, "We would be happy to share some with you." Elizabeth bagged up twelve cookies, and they sent him happily on his way.

14

Elizabeth thought about Mr. Jakes's wanting the cookies and she suddenly had a wonderful idea.

"Nana!" Elizabeth exclaimed excitedly, "I want to have a cookie stand right in your front yard. I will build it and have the sign man down the street make some beautiful signs. We can make your sandcastle cookies to sell to the tourists and neighbors!"

Nana said, "What a wonderful idea, Elizabeth! Your Aunt Jenny has had an old buckboard pony cart in her barn for years. We could paint and decorate it. It would be perfect for displaying baskets of cookies and cold milk. But starting a business is a lot of work. Are you up to the task?"

"Oh, yes!" said Elizabeth.

17

$\mathscr{N}$ana called her sister, who lived a mile down the road. After asking if they could stop by, Elizabeth and Nana headed over to see what Aunt Jenny had in her barn.

"Hi, sis!" said Nana. "Elizabeth is going to start a cookie business, and we'd like to paint your old pony cart and use it as a cookie stand."

18

"What?" said Aunt Jenny in disbelief. "That's a silly idea! A child starting a business? Who will buy the supplies and gamble their money on such a waste of time? Nobody's going to buy cookies from an old pony cart, especially in this town."

Elizabeth started to feel discouraged. She sat down on a bale of hay with her face in her hands. "Nana?" she asked, "do you think it's a waste of time to start a cookie business?"

"What do you think, Elizabeth?" Nana replied.

Elizabeth thought for a while. "I don't care if we sell only one cookie," she told Nana finally. "I have my $10 birthday money to buy the supplies and I want to at least give it a try."

"That's the attitude, Elizabeth!" said Nana. "Don't let someone make you doubt your ideas and dreams. It's better to have tried and failed than not to have tried at all. That's how you learn your best lessons in life."

So Nana and
Elizabeth painted
and decorated
the old pony cart.
They stopped by
the sign man's shop
to pick up the signs,
then they shopped
for ingredients.

Elizabeth
was so
excited
that she
would
have her
own business
—and she was
only eleven years old!

The next morning, Nana and Elizabeth got up extra early and started baking cookies. By eleven o'clock, Elizabeth was ready with $5.00 in change in her cash box, miniature milk cartons on ice, and ten dozen of Nana's Chocolate Maple Sandcastles. Meanwhile, Nana kept baking so the wonderful aroma would loft down the street.

At first no one showed up. Elizabeth started to feel that maybe Aunt Jenny was right, when all of a sudden Mr. Jakes came over. He was so happy to see the delicious cookies for sale that he bought two dozen and went to call all of his friends to share the news about Elizabeth's cookie stand. Before long, customers were standing in line for Elizabeth's cookies. She kept the business open for five hours that first day, closing up just in time for tea.

As Nana prepared
the tea, Elizabeth
sat on the front
porch and, after
taking out the $5.00
in change she started
with, counted the
day's proceeds.

"Nana, look," she
said excitedly.
"We've got $82.50!"

"Now, Elizabeth," replied Nana, "the way to tell how much you have really earned is by keeping very careful records of what you have spent. Look what I got for you."

Nana pulled out a notebook with lined pages, and Elizabeth carefully wrote down her expenses:

Expenses

Ingredients for 10 dozen cookies .. $7.00
Signs from the sign man 15.00
Bags for the cookies 2.00
25 miniature cartons of milk 6.25
$30.25

"Now let's subtract the $30.25 from your total earnings of $82.50, and you have a profit of $52.25. Not bad for your very first day in business, I'd say!"

Elizabeth was learning the lesson of a lifetime. "Not bad for *our* first day!" she said.

$\mathcal{S}$oon everyone in the small town knew about Nana and Elizabeth's cookies, and every day they sold more and more—even some to Aunt Jenny.

"Nana, this has been the best summer of all," Elizabeth said, as she packed up to go home. "Can we do this again next summer? We could add another kind of cookie and give people a choice. I've got so many ideas that I just can't wait!"

"Of course we can," said Nana. She was so proud of her granddaughter and was just as excited about next summer as Elizabeth was.

The
End

Everything in life starts with one idea.

No matter how young children are, they can learn responsibility. Taking an idea from beginning to end takes responsibility, integrity, and character. Failures are just as educational as successes and should be made fun. I believe that inspiring children to be entrepreneurial is the best way to teach any academic subject. It gives them an appreciation of value and work and a reason to put reading, writing, and math to use. It also enables them to mature with character. Today's American youth are bored with meaningless distractions. We are losing the foundation of quality on which America was built. Let's plant their feet in fertile soil and let them blossom with self-respect, confidence, industry, and fun.

—Dianne Linderman